Fur, Feathers, and Flippers

How Animals Live Where They Do

by PATRICIA LAUBER

SCHOLASTIC INC.
New York

Photo Credits

Front cover: © Don Enger/ Animals, Animals
Back cover: © Bruno J. Zehnder/ Peter Arnold Inc.
Title page: © Stephen J. Krasemann/ Photo Researchers Inc.

Animal Homes
P. 4: © Hans & Judy Beste/Animals, Animals. P. 5: © Francois Gohier/Photo Researchers Inc.

The Seas of Antarctica
Pp. 6–7: © David C. Fritts/Earth Scenes. P. 8: *top* © Tom McHugh/ Photo Researchers Inc.; *bottom* © M.A. Chappell/Animals, Animals. P. 9: © Rosemary Chastney/Ocean Images, Inc. P. 10: *top* © Kooyman/Animals, Animals; *bottom* © Arthur Holzman/Animals, Animals. P. 11: *top* © J. Brandt/ Animals, Animals; *bottom* © John Boyd/Animals, Animals. P. 12: ©

Kooyman/Animals, Animals. P. 13: © Kooyman/Animals, Animals.

The Grasslands of Africa
P. 14: © S. Dalton/Photo Researchers Inc. Pp. 14–15: © Stephen J. Krasemann/Photo Researchers Inc. P. 16: © Sven-Olof Lindblad/Photo Researchers Inc. P. 17: *top* © Leonard Lee Rue III/Animals, Animals; *bottom* © Stephen J. Krasemann/DRK Photo. P. 18: *top* © Stephen J. Krasemann/Peter Arnold Inc.; *bottom* © Terry Murphy/Animals, Animals. P. 19: © Anup & Manoj Shah/ Animals, Animals. P. 20: © Anup & Manoj Shah/Animals, Animals. P. 21: © Gregory Dimijiah/Photo Researchers Inc.

The Forests of New England
P. 22: © Jerry Howard/Positive Images. Pp. 22–23: © Fred Curran/

f/Stop Pictures Inc. P. 24: *top* © Ken Cole/Animals, Animals; *bottom* © John Gerlach/DRK Photo. P. 25: © Jerry Howard/Positive Images. P. 26: © Carl R. Sams II/Peter Arnold Inc. P. 27: *top* © Pat & Tom Leeson/Photo Researchers Inc.; *bottom* © Ralph A. Reinhold/ Animals, Animals. P. 28: © Len Rue Jr./Animals, Animals. P. 29: © Steve Maslowski/Photo Researchers Inc.

The Desert of the Southwest
P. 30: © Robert P. Comport/ Earth Scenes. Pp. 30–31: © Jerry L. Ferrara/Photo Researchers Inc. P. 32: © Mickey Gibson/Earth Scenes. P. 33: *left* © W. H. Hodge/ Peter Arnold Inc.; *right* © John Gerlach/Earth Scenes. P. 34: © Ray Richardson/Animals, Animals. P. 35: *top* © Wyman Meinzer/ Peter Arnold Inc.; *bottom* © Joe

McDonald/Peter Arnold Inc.; *right* © Craig K. Lorenz/Photo Researchers Inc. P. 36: © E. R. Degginger/ Animals, Animals. P. 37: © Craig K. Lorenz/Photo Researchers Inc.

The Tundra of the Far North
Pp. 38–39: © Brian Milne/Earth Scenes. P. 40: © Stephen J. Krasemann/Peter Arnold Inc. P. 41: *left* © Tom McHugh/Photo Researchers Inc.; *bottom right* © John Bova/ Photo Researchers Inc.; *top right* © Breck P. Kent/Animals, Animals. P. 42: © Stephen J. Krasemann/ Peter Arnold Inc. P. 43: © Ted Kerasote/Photo Researchers Inc. P. 44: *top* © Francisco Erize/Bruce Coleman Inc.; *bottom* © Fred Bruemmer/Peter Arnold Inc. P. 45: © Yogi, Inc./Peter Arnold Inc. P. 47: © Richard Kolar/Animals, Animals.

Title page: African hunting dogs roam the grasslands by day. They are runners that hunt prey, usually antelope, in packs.

Library of Congress Cataloging-in-Publication Data
Lauber, Patricia.
Fur, feathers, and flippers: how animals live where they do / by Patricia Lauber.
p.   cm.
ISBN 0-590-45071-9
1. Habitat (Ecology)—Juvenile literature. 2. Zoogeography—Juvenile literature.
[1. Habitat (Ecology) 2. Animal distribution.]
I. Title.
QH541.14.L37   1994
591.5—dc20   93-40915
CIP
AC

12 11 10 9 8 7 6 5 4 3 2 1   4 5 6 7 8 9/9
Printed in the U.S.A.   37

First printing, November 1994
Photo research by Grace How
Book design by David Turner

Contents

Animal Homes

The house mouse can live almost anywhere that people can live. It makes its home in our houses and eats what we eat. It also eats a lot of things we don't, such as the glue that holds books together.

The koala lives in the wild only in Australia. It finds food, water, and shelter in eucalyptus trees, where it sleeps and rests eighteen to twenty hours a day. At night it feeds on eucalyptus leaves. It is a picky eater. Australia has about five hundred kinds of eucalyptus trees. Koalas eat the leaves of only six. Koalas do not drink water. They get moisture from the dew on leaves and from the leaves themselves.

Few animals have the special needs of a koala. Few can eat as many foods and live in as many places as the house mouse. Most are somewhere in between. All need food, but they can eat several kinds. Some travel with the seasons to find what they need — more food, a warmer climate, a place to lay their eggs or give birth to their young. Some have ways of living in one place all year-round.

There is a special name for the kind of place in which an animal can live. It is called the animal's habitat.

Left A young koala clings to its mother in a eucalyptus tree. Like kangaroos, koalas are pouched mammals. At birth, a baby is tiny, less than an inch long. It lives in its mother's pouch for the first eight months. After that, it travels on her back or is hugged close to her chest at rest.

Right Humpback whales often breach — they hurl themselves out of the water, twist their bodies in the air, and land with a crash like thunder.

The habitat of a gray squirrel, for example, is among trees. There the squirrel finds nuts, seeds, and fruits to eat. It finds shelter in the hollows of tree trunks or among the branches. It has a safe place to raise its young.

Oceans are the habitat of whales. Most of the big whales spend the summer feeding in cold waters of the far north or far south. In winter, they move to warmer waters, where the young are born.

No matter where they live, all animals depend on green plants for food. This is as true of whales as it is of squirrels. The reason is that only green plants can make their own food. Some animals eat plants or plant parts. Some eat animals that eat plants. And some eat both.

Wherever green plants grow, some animals can live. There are animals in deserts, lakes and oceans, and forests. There are animals on hot plains and on cold lands near the poles. Each kind is suited, or adapted, to the place where it lives. Animals and their habitats fit together like the pieces of a jigsaw puzzle.

The Seas of Antarctica

A white continent lies at the far south of the world, at the South Pole. Its name is Antarctica, and its color comes from the ice cap that covers nearly all of it. In places, the ice is more than two miles thick. It is made of snows that fell over millions of years and did not melt away.

The heart of Antarctica is the coldest place in the world. In winter, temperatures fall far below zero. Winds howl across the ice. Skies are dark, because the South Pole is pointing away from the sun. The heartland is cold even in summer, when the South Pole points toward the sun. The sun is always low in the sky. Its rays are spread out and weak.

Antarctica is too cold and icy to be home to much year-round life. It has a few simple plants, such as mosses, which grow in sheltered bare spots. A few small animals live among the plants. They are insects and mites, none as big as a housefly. They survive the cold because their bodies make a kind of antifreeze.

Yet in summer, the waters off Antarctica are alive with animals. The waters are a rich feeding ground for animals that find their food in the sea and are adapted to cold.

In the sea, as on the land, animals depend on green plants. The plants appear in spring, when the winter-frozen seas break up, and ice is carried away by winds and currents. Billions upon billions of tiny green plants float to the surface of the open water.

The water holds minerals and gases that green plants need to make food. Spring brings sunlight, which green plants use as energy in making food. By summer, there is almost no darkness. The green plants multiply quickly. So do the tiny animals that feed on them and on one another. Among the

tiny animals are krill, which look like shrimp. By summer, huge patches of water are red with krill.

Krill are food for some of the biggest animals on earth — blue whales, finbacks, humpbacks, and right whales. Every year giant whales spend the summer off Antarctica, feasting on krill near the floating ice, or pack ice.

Whales that feed on krill have no teeth. Instead, each has what looks like a huge mustache growing from its upper jaw. The mustache is made of a material like our fingernails. It is

Antarctica is the continent at the far south of the world. The Antarctic is the region of land, ice, ocean, and islands around the South Pole. It lies south of an area where cold water moving north from the Antarctic Ocean sinks below the warmer waters of the Atlantic, Pacific, and Indian oceans. The area where the cold and warmer waters come together, or converge, is called the Antarctic Convergence. It marks the boundary of the Antarctic.

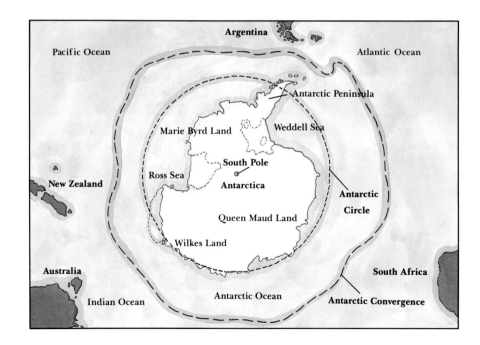

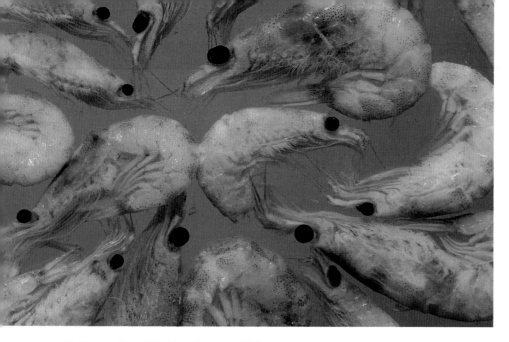

Krill are 2 to 3 inches long. Thick swarms of them form the main food of baleen whales, crabeater seals, squid, and many fishes and birds of the Antarctic.

called baleen. A whale uses its baleen as a strainer. It swims through swarms of krill and small fish, taking a big mouthful of food and water. Then it presses the water out. The food is trapped and swallowed.

Whales with teeth also spend the summer near Antarctica, feeding on fish and other animals that feed on krill. Only one of the toothed whales is a giant — the sperm whale. It dives as deep as a mile to catch squid, which are relatives of the octopus.

Baleen whales do most of their feeding in summer. They build up a thick layer of fat, called blubber. During the rest of the year, their bodies draw on blubber for energy.

Although they live in the sea, whales are not fish. They are mammals, just as we are. They nurse their young on milk.

They breathe air. And they are warm-blooded — their bodies make heat. That is another reason why whales need blubber. Blubber seals in their body heat and keeps it from being lost to cold water.

Seals are also mammals that live in the sea. Unlike whales, they can haul out onto land or ice. Two kinds often seen near Antarctica are Weddell and leopard seals.

A Weddell seal is a gentle, tubby animal that weighs up to nine hundred pounds. A quarter of its weight is blubber. In summer, Weddells haul out onto pack ice, where they sleep for hours. Each has a hole in the ice that lets it slide into the water, where it dives to find fish and squid. After a dive, the seal surfaces at its hole to breathe.

Other seals swim north to escape the bitter cold and gale winds of winter. Weddell seals go under the sea ice that is

Right The open mouth of a humpback whale shows the fringe of baleen that hangs from its upper jaw. When the mouth closes and water is pressed out, food is trapped behind the baleen.

Below Weddell seals spend much of their time resting and sleeping on pack ice.

attached to Antarctica. The water is warmer than the air, and they are sheltered from the wind. They keep their breathing holes open by gnawing and scraping at the ice.

Leopard seals have sleek bodies built for speed. They have sharp teeth set in huge jaws that open wide. They can use their teeth to strain krill from water. But leopard seals also eat fish, squid, young crabeater seals, and birds, among them penguins.

Several kinds of penguins nest in the far south. Only two lay their eggs on or near the main part of Antarctica. They

Swimming under the ice, a photographer took this picture of a Weddell seal and its breathing hole.

The leopard seal preys on many other animals of the Antarctic.

are the Adélie and emperor penguins. Like all birds, penguins are warm-blooded. Unlike most birds, penguins cannot fly. But they are expert swimmers, soaring through the water as other birds soar through the air.

Adélies winter on pack ice north of Antarctica, where they spend much of their time fattening up on krill. Fat helps to seal in an Adélie's body heat. So do its feathers, which are short and tightly packed together. They form a thick coat that keeps water away from the body. Tufts of down grow from the base of each feather. The down acts as an undershirt that traps warm air close to the body. Almost no heat escapes — snow that falls on an Adélie does not melt.

With the coming of spring, Adélies set out for Antarctica. Once ashore, each heads for its old nesting ground, a piece of bare ground where snow has melted or been blown away. There, mates build a nest of pebbles.

Top An Adélie penguin checks the eggs in its nest of pebbles.

Bottom On snow and ice, the penguins have two ways of moving. They waddle along until their walking muscles tire. Then they flop on their bellies and toboggan, kicking with their feet and "rowing" with their flippers.

Once a female has laid her two blue-white eggs, she goes off to feed in the sea. The male takes over the nest. He keeps the eggs warm and guards them against enemies. The worst enemy is the skua, a big brown bird that looks like a gull. It is one of many seabirds that fly far south each summer to nest and raise their young. Skuas build their nests near colonies of penguins. Whenever they can, they steal and eat penguin eggs and chicks.

When the female Adélie returns, she takes over the nest. Her mate goes off to feed. From then on they take turns. After the eggs hatch, parents must also feed the chicks. Young Adélies cannot swim and feed themselves until they have grown warm, waterproof feathers. They are ready to go to sea in late summer. Then, like their parents, they spend the winter on pack ice.

In autumn, days grow short. Temperatures fall. The seas begin to freeze. This is the time when emperor penguins return to lay their eggs and raise their young during an Antarctic winter. Only a very large penguin has enough body fat to do this — and emperors are the biggest of all. They stand nearly four feet tall and weigh as much as seventy pounds.

Colonies of emperors gather on the sea ice near shore. They do not build nests. Instead, a month after arriving, a female lays a big, pale-green egg on the ice. She works it onto her feet and lowers her belly to cover and warm it. A few hours

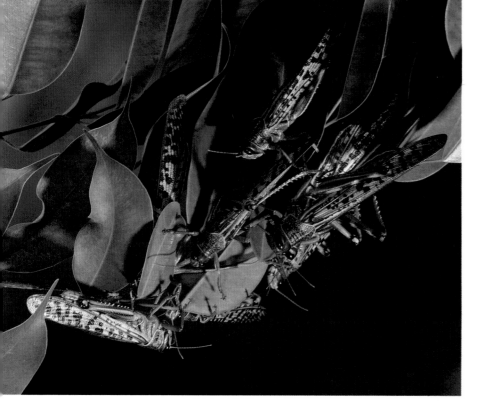

Much of East Africa lies on or near the equator. Here every day is hot, because the sun rises high in the sky all year-round. Seasons are either rainy or dry. There are times when rains fall for weeks or months. There are times when little or no rains fall for three to eight months.

Grass grows better than other plants in a climate like this. During a dry season, grass dies back, but when the rains come again, grass springs up again, from its roots.

Most plants grow from the tips of leaves or shoots, but grass grows from the base of its leaves. This means it grows back quickly after being grazed.

That is why the plains of East Africa are seas of green or golden grass, with scattered trees. That is why they are home to millions of grass-eating animals — and to meat-eaters that prey on the grass-eaters.

The Grasslands of Africa

...later the male takes the egg, balancing it on his feet and covering it with a fold of belly skin. Now the female goes off to feed on fish, squid, and krill. She may cross sixty miles of ice to reach open water.

In winter, no other animals are around to prey on penguin eggs, but the cold is dangerous. Male emperors huddle together, keeping themselves and their eggs warm even when temperatures drop to forty or sixty degrees below zero Fahrenheit.

Females return two months later, just as the chicks hatch. Each finds her own mate and chick. She forces up food for the chick. Now it is the male's turn to feed at sea. He has spent more than three months without eating and has lost nearly half his body weight. Once he returns, the parents take turns feeding the chick and keeping it warm.

In spring, the sea ice breaks up. The young emperors are ready to float away with it, for they have grown their adult feathers. Now half the size of their parents, they will finish growing up on the pack ice. The young birds will find plenty of food because, with the coming of spring, billions of tiny green plants are multiplying — as are the tiny animals that feed on them.

Left Adélies pop out of the water onto a piece of pack ice.

Right When an emperor chick is small, it keeps warm under a parent's belly. When it outgrows this cozy place, it may still try to cram itself in.

Grasshoppers are some of the smallest grass-eaters. A grasshopper chops off a blade of grass, then uses its front legs to push the blade into its mouth. Grasshoppers are everywhere in the grass, and almost all the insect-eaters catch grasshoppers when they can. But it's not easy to spot a grasshopper. Grasshoppers may be the same color or pattern as the plants they are on. Cattle egrets and some other birds find grasshoppers by following large, hoofed mammals. As the mammals

Left Grasshoppers are small plant-eaters that are food for many other animals.

Right Most of East Africa is a high plateau. But the region also holds the highest mountain in all of Africa and the largest, deepest lakes. There are deserts, thorny bushlands, rolling grasslands, grasslands dotted with trees, and mountains with wet moors and forests. The land offers habitats for many kinds of animals.

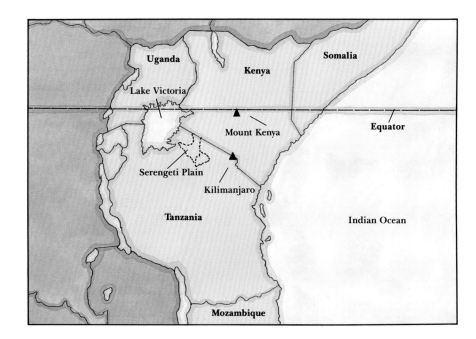

walk, their feet stir the grass. The grasshoppers fly up into the air and are seized by the birds.

Hares and rabbits are small mammals that eat grass. Several kinds of rats also eat grass, or grass and seeds. These animals are, in turn, eaten by many birds of prey and by jackals, bat-eared foxes, and wildcats, among others. In fact, some kind of bird, mammal, or snake feeds on everything that creeps, hops, or scurries through the grass.

The seas of grass are also home to the biggest herds of hoofed mammals in the world. In places, a million or more of these animals are moving about and feeding on grass. East Africa has more than sixty kinds of antelope, such as gazelles, wildebeests, topis, and elands. It has zebras. It has buffaloes. It has giraffes and elephants, which usually feed on the leaves of trees and bushes, but also eat grass.

These many big grass-eaters can share a habitat because they do not compete. Zebras, wildebeests, and topis may graze together. They eat the same kinds of grass, but they do not eat the same parts. Zebras eat the tough, outer part of the stem. Then topis, which have pointed muzzles, can reach the lower parts. Wildebeests, which have square muzzles, bite off the leaves that grow sideways. Together these animals clip grass down to its base. Cutting grass causes it to grow. A few days later, Thomson's gazelles are nibbling the tender new growth.

Left Wildebeests are plant-eaters that feed on grasses, bushes, and the juicy plants called succulents. They migrate with the seasons to find food. In late May or early June, they set out for their dry-season grazing grounds, where they also find shade and water. Huge herds travel in long columns on a journey that covers 150 miles. Wildebeests are also called gnus.

Topis also eat grass that has reached its full height and dried out. New blades grow and are eaten by other animals. Elephants tear off long, tough grasses, leaving short grasses that other animals use.

Most of the big grass-eaters move around to seek food, traveling as much as one thousand miles a year. Their long legs and small, hard hoofs are well suited to crossing the dry plains. Their long legs also make them speedy runners and help them escape from the meat-eaters of the plains.

Lions are the chief hunters on the plains. They kill the biggest prey and harvest the most meat. These big cats eat antelopes, buffaloes, zebras, and even giraffes. But they usually take what they can easily catch.

Most often, lions hunt by night in groups of one or more families. They may stalk a zebra or a wildebeest through tall grass, taking hours to close in on one animal. To catch a speedy gazelle, they must take it by complete surprise in a short, quick dash.

The leopard is next in size to the lion. Leopards hunt alone at night, usually in forests or wooded places near the plains. They attack from hiding. After eating, a leopard may drag its catch up into a tree, to be finished later. When leopards do hunt on the plains, they feed on the newborn young of hoofed mammals. Many kinds of young are able to walk minutes after birth. But they cannot run fast enough to escape a leopard.

Top Topis are able to share grazing land with wildebeests because the two do not eat the same parts of grass.

Bottom The calves of wildebeests are born able to see and to struggle to their feet. Minutes later, they are able to travel with their mothers. They nurse for seven or eight months, but start to eat grass at one week old.

Top   Swiftest of all land animals, the cheetah can run as fast as 70 miles an hour over short distances.

Bottom   African hunting dogs chase prey until it tires; then they attack.

The cheetah is the third of the big cats. It hunts by day, first stalking a small antelope, then running it down. The cheetah is the fastest runner of all land animals.

Two other animals also prey on the grazing animals. One is the African hunting dog. Hunting dogs are long-distance runners that hunt in packs by day. Their leader chooses a prey animal, usually an antelope. The pack chases the animal until it tires; then the pack attacks. Hunting dogs are fierce — even a leopard will scramble out of their way.

The spotted hyena is the other hunter. These hyenas hunt by night, moving about until they spot prey. They yap and snap at a herd until they can single out a sick animal or a young one. Then the whole pack attacks.

The hyenas seldom leave any scraps, because their jaws and teeth can cut through almost anything. But the other big hunters do. A cheetah, for example, eats only the meat of its prey and leaves the rest. The remains become food for the animals that usually feed on what others have killed. The name for such animals is scavengers.

Although the spotted hyena is a hunter, two other kinds of hyenas are scavengers, coming out at night to feed on what the big cats have killed. A

Right   Most often, lions hunt at night. Some hunt alone, others in family groups, working together to stalk prey. Lions also steal food from cheetahs, hyenas — and other lions.

Left A leopard takes its ease in a tree, where it may also store part of a kill for future eating.

Right Burchell's zebra travel in herds. Some members act as sentries while others drink.

single hyena must wait until a lion has finished eating. But a pack of hyenas — yapping, snarling, dashing in and out — can drive a lion away from its food.

Jackals are also scavengers, as are the big birds called vultures. Vultures find their food by soaring high in the sky and looking down. Their sharp eyes pick out kills on the ground. Sometimes hyenas and jackals watch the flight of vultures, using the birds to lead them to food. On the grasslands of East Africa, nothing goes to waste.

The grass and the animals fit together. Grass grows best when it is cut or grazed. The hoofed mammals graze it. If their numbers multiplied and multiplied, they would graze too much and kill the grass. But this does not happen, because the hunters keep down the number of grazers. If the hunters killed too many grazers, then they would run out of food. But this does not happen either. The hunters never kill for sport, only for food. At times when food is scarce, many young meat-eaters do not live to grow up. So the number of meat-eaters is also kept in check, and the life of the plains is in balance.

The Forests
of New England

New England is a place where trees grow well. The growing season lasts long enough for them to make the food they need. Winters are cold, but only the top few inches of soil ever freeze. Trees can put down deep roots. Water is plentiful. It falls as rain in spring, summer, and autumn and as snow or rain in winter.

That is why New England has forests, which are large areas with thick growths of trees. That is why it has woods, which are smaller areas of trees. Some of the trees are green all year, among them hemlocks and white pines. They shed only some of their needle-shaped leaves at one time. Most of the trees are the kind called broadleafs — maples, beeches, oaks, and others that shed their leaves in autumn.

Leaves are the food factories of trees. Green coloring matter, called chlorophyll, makes the food that trees need to grow

and to form seeds. Leaves and other tree parts are food for many animals of the forest. The trees themselves are nesting places and homes for animals that fly or climb.

Spring brings the forest to life. The sun rises higher in the sky each day, shining through the dark skeletons of broadleaf trees and warming the earth below. Tender green shoots push up into the light. Soon the forest floor is dotted with the pinks, yellows, and blues of wildflowers.

Once flowers begin to bloom, insects appear, feeding on nectar and pollen. Near streams, ponds, and swamps, frogs

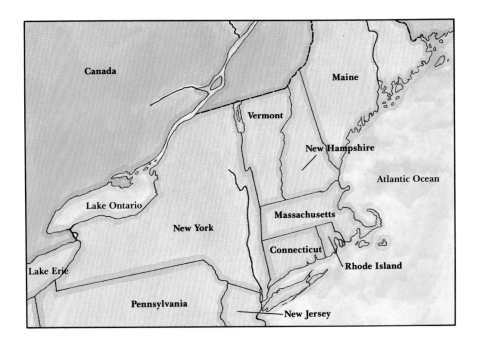

Left   Lady's slippers are among the flowers of spring in New England forests.

Right   The forests of hemlocks, white pines, and broadleaf trees reach from southern Canada through New England and New York into Pennsylvania.

are out and about, catching insects on their sticky tongues. A nightly chorus rises as male frogs call for mates. Salamanders, silent relatives of the frogs, appear about the same time. Most live near water, feeding on worms, insect young, and other small creatures.

The spring sun also brings out reptiles — snakes, turtles, lizards — from their winter dens. Like frogs and salamanders, reptiles cannot make their own body heat. The reptiles of the forest warm up in the sun or on sun-warmed rocks. All eat other animals.

Bats wake from their winter sleep. They swoop through the night air, catching insects. Black bears wake and leave their dens. Cubs, born during winter, follow their mothers on hunts for plant and animal food. Litters of rabbits and hares are being born. And soon there will be young squirrels, chipmunks, skunks, raccoons, opossums, and deer, as well as foxes, weasels, and bobcats.

A few birds live all year in the forest or along its edges. Spring brings thousands of others that have wintered to the south. Some stop for food and rest before flying farther north. Some come to spend the summer and raise their young.

The first arrivals are usually males. Each lays claim to an area where his young can be raised and fed. He defends this

Top   Some beetles feed on leaves.

Bottom   A sure sign of spring is the nightly chorus of spring peepers, calling for mates. Only the males can sing. The tiny frog produces sounds by forcing air from his lungs across his vocal cords to a pouch on his throat. The swelling of the pouch makes the sound louder.

Right   Painted turtles, like other turtles, sleep away the winter and reappear in spring.

place against others of his own kind, because they eat the same food. But he can share with other kinds of birds that do not compete for food. A wood thrush, for example, eats earthworms and other small creatures of the forest floor, as well as berries. It does not compete with a red-eyed vireo, which picks insects from leaves. It does not compete with a woodpecker, which digs insects out of tree bark.

As summer draws closer, a mist of green appears as buds open on shrubs and trees. Then leaves unfold. The forest becomes a world of green, flecked with sunlight. Its floor is cool and dimly lighted.

Like a building, a forest has stories. The top story forms a tent and is called the canopy. It is the place where the tops of trees grow together. Most of the forest's food is made in the canopy, because this is where most of the green leaves are. But the upper side of the canopy is not a good place for animals. The sun is too hot, the rain too heavy, and the winds too strong during a storm.

Farther down in the canopy there is shelter from sun, rain, and wind, and there is plenty of food. Thousands of beetles, bugs, and caterpillars munch steadily on leaves. Aphids suck juices from leaves. All these small plant-eaters are preyed on by other small creatures — spiders, hornets, wasps — and by birds. Warblers, vireos, flycatchers, scarlet tanagers, and other insect-eaters flit among the branches.

Left   **Black bear cubs practice tree climbing.**

The chickadee (*above*) is one of the few birds that live deep in the forest. Most, such as the red-eyed vireo (*below*), build their nests and feed their hungry young in the vines and shrubs near the forest's edge. Chickadees live year-round in New England. Vireos fly south for the winter.

A few mammals make their way into the canopy. Squirrels race through the treetops in search of seeds and nuts. Porcupines may inch their way up to feed on leaves and twigs.

Below the canopy is the understory of the forest. It is made up of smaller trees. Some are young trees that grew from seeds dropped by the tall trees. Some are low-growing trees, such as dogwoods and sassafras. Many birds find the understory good for nesting. The canopy shelters them from storms. It shelters them from hawks and owls, which would prey on them. Yet they are well above the ground, out of reach of other animals that would eat them.

Beneath the understory is the shrub layer. Shrubs are woody plants with several stems, which do not grow as tall as trees. Witch hazel, mountain laurel, and blueberry are all shrubs. Shrubs are often thickest close to the ground, so they offer hiding places for small mammals — shrews, mice, chipmunks — that make their burrows nearby. Some birds nest in shrubs, and ground-nesting birds may make their nests beneath shrubs. The leaves of shrubs are food for insects. Their seeds and berries are autumn food for birds and mammals.

Still lower, nestled against the forest floor, is the herb layer. Herbs are green plants with stems that are soft, not woody. Wildflowers, ferns, and mosses are all herbs. Many animals live in the herb layer — insects and other bugs, mice,

Left   The bobcat hunts mainly at night, taking hares, rabbits, other small mammals, and birds. It may also kill fawns and, in winter, adult deer.

Right   Fawns have spotted coats that help to conceal them on the sun-dappled forest floor.

toads, turtles, and some ground-nesting birds. Fawns lie hidden in the herbs, where their spotted coats blend with flecks of sunlight on the leaves.

At night, meat-eaters set out from their burrows and dens. Owls hunt mice and other small animals. Weasels search for mice, shrews, rabbits, squirrels, young birds, snakes, and just about any other small animal that moves. Young raccoons and skunks follow their mothers, learning to catch insects, mice, snakes, frogs. Bobcats and foxes prowl the forest in search of larger prey.

As summer ends, birds fly south with their young. Days grow shorter. Broadleaf trees no longer make chlorophyll. The green in their leaves breaks down and is not replaced. Now colors that were hidden by the green appear and the forest is ablaze with reds, oranges, yellows, and golds.

Winds blow colder. Animals that cannot make their own heat disappear into their winter dens.

Bears are busily fattening up on autumn nuts and fruits before sleeping away the winter. Squirrels are gathering nuts.

Broadleaf trees are bare. An early snow falls. Winter has come to the forest.

The Desert
of the Southwest

A desert is a dry land, a land where little rain or snow falls. It is a land that receives less than ten inches of water a year — the forests of New England receive four times as much. A few of the world's deserts are cold, among them the icy heart of Antarctica. But many deserts are hot.

The Sonoran desert of Arizona and Mexico is a hot desert. For much of the year, the sun beats down from a bright blue sky. The air shimmers with heat, making distant mountains seem to dance. Months go by without rain. Both spring and early summer are dry. Rain does not come until the middle of summer. Then it falls in violent thunderstorms that drench some parts of the desert but not others. Rain pelts the sunbaked earth. Some of it sinks in, but most of it runs off. Dry streambeds suddenly carry raging torrents of water. Soon the skies clear. A few days later, thunderstorms return.

By late summer, the rains come to an end. Autumn is dry. Early winter is dry. Then rain may come again. This time it falls more gently. All told, the Sonoran desert receives about five inches of water a year. To live here, plants and animals must be adapted to life in a hot, dry land.

After the winter rains, the bare earth of the desert is blanketed with tiny wildflowers. They have grown from seeds that lay dormant, or sleeping, during the dry months. Given

Left Wildflowers carpet the desert, brought to life by the winter rains.

Right Deserts are lands where little rain or snow falls. Most receive water during only one or two months of the year. In some regions, mountains block an ocean's moisture-bearing winds from reaching inland. In others, cold ocean currents cool moisture-bearing winds and rain falls in the ocean, not on the land. These conditions created the Sonoran desert.

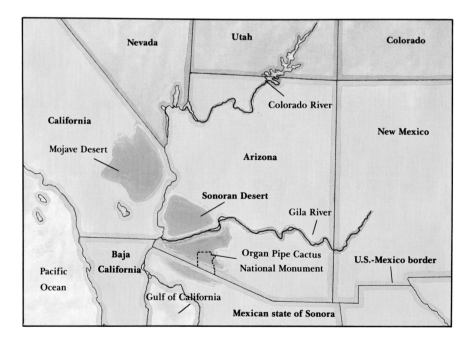

water, seeds sprout, plants grow, flowers bloom, and new seeds form — all within a few weeks. The parent plants die. The ground once more looks bare. But scattered across it are millions of seeds. Many will be eaten by animals. Many will spring to life another year.

Several kinds of woody plants grow in the desert. Mesquite has roots that reach down forty to sixty feet, where they tap underground water. Like all green plants, mesquite gives off water through its green parts. But it has small leaves that fold lengthwise during the day. The folding means that there is less surface area. And that means less water is lost.

During the dry months, creosote's leaves may turn brown and the plant becomes dormant. With the coming of rain, the shrub puts out a new growth of green leaves. The leaves are covered with wax, which cuts down water loss. Creosote never competes with other plants for water, because none can grow near it. Its roots put out a poison that kills other plants.

When there is water, the tiny leaves of the paloverde make food. In the dry months, the paloverde sheds its leaves. But the green bark of the trunk makes enough food to keep the plant alive.

Cactuses survive by storing water. Some fifty kinds, of all shapes, grow in the Sonoran desert. Some look like barrels. Others look like the pipes of an organ, clumps of sticks, or pincushions. A pincushion cactus may be only two inches high. A giant saguaro may be fifty or sixty feet tall. Yet in some ways they are all alike.

Left An organ-pipe cactus stores water in its arms, which are supported inside by a woody framework. The pleated outside skin opens up when the cactus has a chance to absorb water. The plant can grow to 20 feet tall.

A cactus has a network of shallow, wide-spreading roots. They soak up large amounts of water when rain falls. The water is stored in the plant's pulpy flesh, which acts like a sponge. Some cactuses, such as the saguaro, have pleats. These open up and let the plant store even more water.

Although they are green plants, cactuses have no leaves. They make their food in their trunks and branches. These parts have a thick, waxy skin.

The skin bristles with sharp spines, which cast tiny shadows. Together the thousands of tiny shadows shade the skin from the hot sun.

The saguaro (*right*) is a giant cactus, which may grow 50 or 60 feet tall. The pincushion cactus (*below*) is only inches high.

Red-tailed hawks fly high above the desert, where the air is cooler. They make their nests near the tops of big saguaros.

Animals also have ways of surviving in a hot land. On a summer day, jackrabbits may bound across the desert. But most of the animals are still, for the heat is great. By early afternoon, the air temperature five feet above the ground may be 125 degrees. One foot above the ground it is 150 degrees. The surface of the desert may be 180 degrees. Coyotes sit or nap in the shade of shrubs and trees. Small animals take shelter in their burrows. Ground squirrels sleep away the hottest part of the year, just as other animals sleep away winter in cold parts of the world.

Birds are the most active daytime animals. They can fly above the hot ground and perch in high places. The red-tailed hawk swoops down to catch rats, mice, and lizards that have strayed from their burrows. The Gila woodpecker is out and about, tapping at a saguaro in search of food. It is looking for the young of insects that laid their eggs in the cactus. This is helpful to the saguaro. Left uneaten, the insect young would injure or even kill the big cactus.

Woodpeckers also carve out nest holes in saguaros. The plants heal themselves. Sap forms a hard shell around the hole and keeps water from escaping. Woodpeckers make new nest holes every year. When they have raised their young and moved on, the holes become nests for other birds — sparrow hawks, screech owls, elf owls, flycatchers.

By late afternoon, the desert is cooling off. More animals appear. One of them is the roadrunner, a bird named for its habit of sprinting along highways. It eats insects and the lizards and snakes that come out as the ground cools.

Two of the desert lizards are plant-eaters, feeding on leaves, flowers, and cactus fruits in spring and summer. They spend the cooler months sleeping underground. Most of the other lizards feed on insects — ants, beetles, flies. The biggest lizard, the twenty-four-inch-long Gila monster, also eats the eggs of snakes and birds.

All the snakes are meat-eaters. Most feed on insects, mice, and lizards. The diamondback rattlesnake can also swallow gophers and jackrabbits. In turn, snakes are eaten by roadrunners, hawks, owls, and other snakes.

Early evening is a time when animals visit streams or places where water seeps out of the ground. Only a few desert animals can live without drinking water. The grasshopper

Top   The roadrunner chases its prey on the ground and swallows much of its food whole. It is about sixteen inches long and a rapid runner.

Right   Every year, a Gila woodpecker chops out a new nest hole in a saguaro. It does not carry nesting material into the hole and build a nest. The hole itself serves as the nest.

Bottom   The two-foot-long Gila monster is the biggest lizard in North America. It eats bird and lizard eggs, young birds, and small rodents.

mouse, for example, gets water by eating juicy plants or prey. The kangaroo rat is able to live on dry food, without drinking. Bounding along on its hindlegs, it searches out seeds, stems, and leaves. It uses its short front legs to stuff food into its cheek pockets.

Night brings out many small animals. Some desert plants open their flowers at night. Moths are busy feeding at them. Bats and nighthawks feed on flying insects. On the ground, mice and wood rats scurry about in search of seeds.

To the coyote, evening and night mean food. It eats cactus fruits and almost any animal it can catch. As the sun goes down, the coyote goes hunting. Badgers leave their own burrows and start digging out gophers and rock squirrels. The kit fox also leaves its burrow. Its favorite prey is the kangaroo rat, although it also eats insects, wood rats, small birds, lizards, and even scorpions.

As the night ends, many of the animals again visit places where they can drink. The sky turns pink as the sun edges up. Once more it is time to take shelter from the heat of the day.

The Tundra of the Far North

A white sea lies at the far north of the world, at the North Pole. Its name is the Arctic Ocean, and its color comes from the grinding, shifting sheets of ice that cover almost all of it. Even in summer, the ice does not melt away.

The ocean is nearly surrounded by land that stretches around the world. It is land that receives little water — it is a cold desert. Together, the ocean and the northern lands are known as the Arctic.

Some people say that the Arctic begins at the Arctic Circle. But the Arctic Circle is a line drawn on maps. It does not appear on the ground. The climate does not change from one side of it to the other. Animals know nothing about it. Scientists who study plants and animals describe the Arctic in a different way. They say it is the northland where trees cannot grow, except in sheltered valleys.

Trees cannot grow for several reasons. Summers are too short and cool for them to make the food they need. Apart from the top few inches, the ground is frozen year-round. Trees cannot put down roots. Soils are poor. If a tree seed sprouts, it may take a hundred years to grow knee-high.

The edge of an area where trees will not grow is called the tree line. It is not a neat, straight boundary. As forests reach north, they thin out. Trees become stunted, then disappear. Some kinds of animals live south of the tree line, in forests. Some live north of the tree line, on the open rolling land called tundra. A few move back and forth as seasons and food supplies change.

The tundra is new ground. For thousands of years it was covered by sheets of ice. That ice has melted only in recent times. Today some tundra is bare. Some is carpeted with small

plants — mosses, lichens, grasses, sedges, and tufts of herbs that flower in spring and bear berries in autumn. Most are plants that come up year after year. They are plants that can live with little rain, plants that can freeze without dying. They are plants that can get an early start, growing under the snows of winter. And they are plants that hug the ground, where temperatures are warmer than in the air above.

An ocean, not a continent, lies at the North Pole. Most of the ocean is covered with ice all year. It is ringed by land where trees cannot grow — by tundra. There the growing season is short, the winters are severe, and little rain or snow falls. Even in summer, when the North Pole points toward the sun and days are long, the sun never rises high in the sky. Its rays never beat down on the tundra, as they do on land to the south. In winter, when the pole points away from the sun, days are short and nights are long on the tundra.

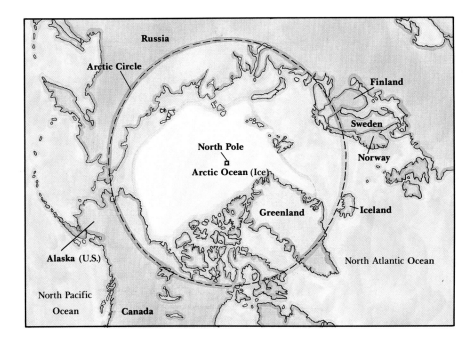

When summer comes to the tundra, the eggs of insects and bugs hatch out. Beetles, springtails, weevils, and caterpillars feed on plants. Other beetles, spiders, and mites prey on the plant-eaters. In June and July, huge clouds of mosquitoes rise from lakes and ponds, where eggs have hatched into young. As the mosquitoes disappear in August, swarms of black flies take their place.

Millions of birds fly to the far north to mate and raise their young. All are birds that nest on the ground or in shrubs. Snow geese are the first to arrive. They are followed by other geese, ducks, and whistling swans. Sandpipers and plovers arrive. So do owls, redpolls, longspurs, snow buntings, horned larks, and many others.

The many kinds of birds find many kinds of food, in ponds and lakes, on the land, and in the air. The birds called turnstones turn over stones to feed on the tiny animals hidden beneath them. On ponds, the little northern phalarope spins like a top, stirring up insects and other small animals from the bottom.

A few kinds of mammals live year-round on the tundra. There are meadow mice, called voles, and their relatives, the lemmings. There are Arctic hares and small herds of big, shaggy musk oxen. There are some barren-ground caribou, although most of these animals winter to the south. In northern Europe, these caribou have been partly tamed and are known as reindeer. All of these animals are plant-eaters.

Left Lichens of many kinds and sizes grow in the far north. A lichen is not a single plant but consists of two plants: an alga and a fungus. Algae are green plants, which can make their own food. Fungi cannot and get their food from the algae. But fungi store water, which the algae need to make food. Each benefits from growing closely with the other.

One meat-eater is the short-tailed weasel, or ermine, which preys on voles and lemmings. Arctic foxes feed on voles, lemmings, and hares. And there are wolves, which can bring down the biggest plant-eaters of all, the musk oxen and caribou.

With the coming of spring, other mammals appear on the tundra. Grizzly bears leave their winter dens to the south and lumber across the tundra, looking for food. They eat almost anything — grasses, berries, fish, birds, mammals. Ground squirrels pop out of burrows in the banks of rivers and lakes, in search of plant food. And thousands of caribou stream onto the tundra from the south, sometimes traveling hundreds of miles. They have long legs and big hoofs, which are split in two.

Top right Snow geese, traveling in V-shaped flights, arrive in the far north to mate and raise their young.

Bottom right A turnstone shows how it earned its name, by turning over stones to find food.

Bottom left Lemmings bear several litters a year, in spring, summer, and even winter. These small rodents are a major food source for meat-eaters of the Arctic.

The hoofs spread out as a caribou walks and keep it from sinking into newly thawed, wet ground.

Lichens are the main food of caribou. But in summer they also eat fresh green sedges, the leaves of shrubs, and tender flowering plants. Calves are born in June, even though the ground is still snowy and temperatures drop below freezing. Many can wobble to their feet twenty minutes after birth, and they are soon able to keep up with the herd.

Summer is short in the Arctic. By late August, birds are leaving. Their young have grown quickly and are ready to fly south. Some will fly as far as Africa. One, the Arctic tern, flies all the way south for the Antarctic summer.

Ground squirrels return to their burrows. Grizzlies head south to their dens. Most of the caribou also move south, followed by packs of wolves.

By October, winter's silence lies upon the tundra. Voles and lemmings take shelter from the bitter cold by living under the snow. They tunnel about, feeding on bark, roots, and other plant parts. Ermines dig them up and eat them. When they tunnel to the surface, they may become food for a fox or a snowy owl, one of the few birds that winters on the tundra.

Left The Arctic fox has a thick layer of underhair, which traps body heat in winter. The underhair is protected by an outer layer of coarse, oily guard hairs, which serve as a waterproof cover.

Right Many caribou live year-round in the woods of the far north. But thousands of others migrate in early summer, streaming onto the tundra, where their young are born. Later, they head south again.

The Arctic hare (*top left*) and the musk ox (*bottom left*) are two mammals that are able to winter in the far north.

Right The snowy owl is one of a few birds that is able to winter in the Arctic.

The ptarmigan is another bird that winters in the Arctic, feeding on the buds of stunted willows. Like the owl, it is kept warm by its feathers. A thick coat of down traps its body heat, and a thick coat of outer feathers keeps it dry. Unlike the owl, the ptarmigan grows feathers on its feet. The feathers act like snowshoes on top of the snow.

The huge hind feet of Arctic hares also act as snowshoes. Like most mammals of the far north, the hares are kept warm by two coats of fur. Thick, woolly underhair traps body heat. An outer layer of oily hairs keeps them dry.

The Arctic fox grows a thick winter coat that covers even the bottoms of its feet. Its small ears are set close to its head and buried in fur. They do not give off much heat. Denning up to sleep, a fox wraps its bushy tail around its body like a quilt.

Musk oxen have long, thick fur that nearly sweeps the ground. In summer, they feed on plants in low-lying places along rivers and streams. In winter, snowdrifts bury these feeding places, and the short-legged animals find walking hard. The herds move to higher ground, where winds blow away the snow and bare the ground. There they wait out the icy gales and snows of winter in one of the harshest habitats on earth.

Animal Habitats and People

People can live nearly anywhere. We build houses and heat them or cool them. In a cold climate, we wear warm clothes. We may grow some of our food or we may go to a store and buy it. And we can buy food that grew hundreds or thousands of miles away.

Only a few kinds of animals can live all over the world. They are the ones that live with us. Some are ones we want, such as our pets. Others are ones that we don't want, such as the house mouse, brown rat, and cockroach — but they live with us anyway.

Animals in the wild can live only in places they are adapted to. They must have the right kind of habitat, where they find the food and space they need.

Because the number of people keeps growing, we keep taking more and more of the earth for ourselves. We, too, need places to live and food to eat. Often we crowd out the animals. We change or destroy their habitats. When we do, the animals are likely to die out.

Yet one of the things that makes the earth a wonderful place to live is its many kinds of animals — its caribou, whales, lions, giraffes, foxes, rabbits, woodpeckers, frogs, and all the others. To keep them on earth, we need to understand animals and their habitats, why and how animals live where they do. Most of all we need to share with them. When we take everything for ourselves, we are the poorer. But when we share, we are the richer.

Gray whales of the eastern Pacific were almost wiped out by hunting. But they have made a comeback. Today many people find pleasure in watching the whales dive, roll, and pop out of the waters off Baja California, where gray whales spend the winter. Some have learned that people will rub them if they approach boats.

INDEX

Page numbers in bold indicate illustrations.

WITHDRAWN

WITHDRAWN